SPECTRUM®
READERS

LEVEL 2

# DANGER!
## Deadly Animals

By Katharine Kenah

Carson-Dellosa
Publishing

# SPECTRUM®

An imprint of Carson-Dellosa Publishing, LLC
P.O. Box 35665
Greensboro, NC 27425-5665

carsondellosa.com

Printed in the USA. All rights reserved.
ISBN 978-1-62399-148-7

01-002131120

Some small things make you say,
"Come quick! Look at this."
A puppy.
A butterfly.
A starfish.

But some small things make you say,
"Stay away! Do not come near."
Turn the page to meet
some little monsters.

# Blue Poison Dart Frog

Look high in the tree.
What do you see?

The frog that you see is
the color of the sky.
Do not touch it.
Its skin is covered with poison.

# Blue-Ringed Octopus

Look into the tide pool.
What do you see?

The octopus that you see is
no longer than your finger.
Do not touch it.
If its rings are blue, it may bite you.

# Flea

Look on your pet.
What do you see?

The flea that you see is
smaller than a grain of rice.
Do not touch it.
It may bite you.

9

# Fly

Look at your lunch.
What do you see?

The fly that you see is
tasting your lunch.
It is using its feet to taste.
Do not touch it.
Flies carry lots of germs.

# Killer Bee

Look on the flower.
What do you see?

The bee that you see is
a kind of honeybee.
It guards its hive and honey well.
Do not touch one.
Bees like this one sting.

# Hornet

Look under that roof.
What do you see?

The hornet that you see builds a nest.
The nest is shaped like a football.
Hornets make their nests out of paper.
Do not touch one.
A hornet stings again and again.

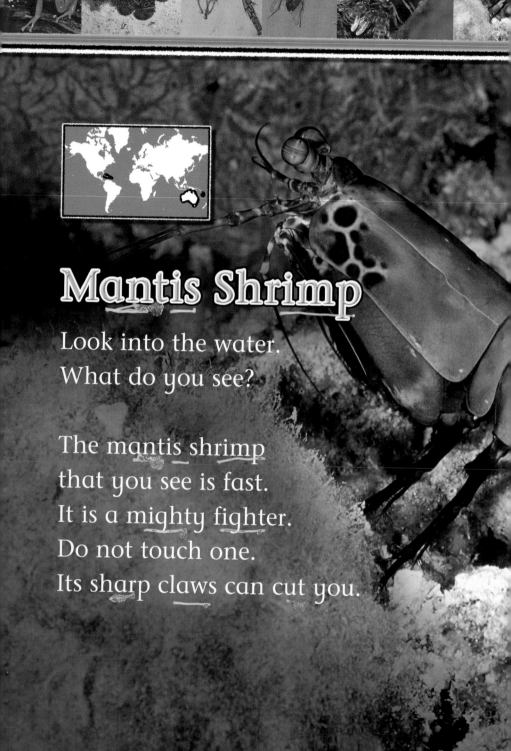

# Mantis Shrimp

Look into the water.
What do you see?

The mantis shrimp
that you see is fast.
It is a mighty fighter.
Do not touch one.
Its sharp claws can cut you.

# Mosquito

Look on your arm.
What do you see?

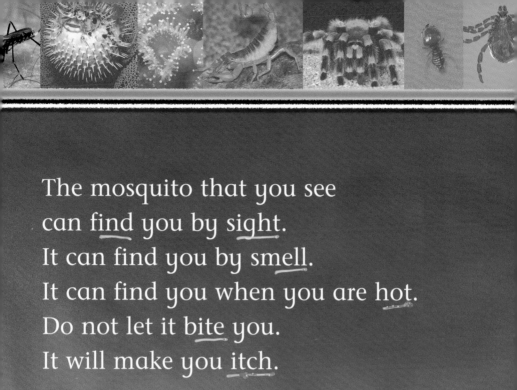

The mosquito that you see
can find you by sight.
It can find you by smell.
It can find you when you are hot.
Do not let it bite you.
It will make you itch.

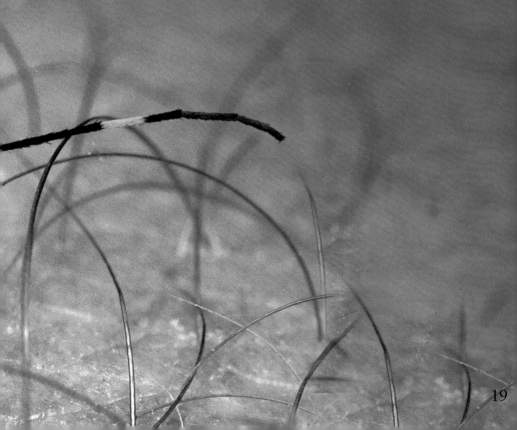

# Puffer Fish

Look into the ocean.
What do you see?

The puffer fish that you see puffs up.
It puffs up when it senses danger.
Do not eat one!
A puffer fish is full of poison.

# Sea Anemone

Look at that coral reef.
What do you see?

The sea anemone that you see
looks like a flower.
It moves in the water to catch food.
Do not touch one.
It will sting you.

# Scorpion

Look on that sunny rock.
What do you see?

The scorpion that you see
likes warm, dark places.
It hunts at night.
Do not touch one.
The scorpion has poison in its tail.

# Tarantula

Look in that hole.
What do you see?

The spider that you see
is a tarantula.
It is as big as a hand.
Do not poke one.
A tarantula will bite you.

# Termite

Look in the wood.
What do you see?

The termite that you see
makes its tall home out of mud.
Termites that live in a group
are called a *colony*.
Do not keep them in your house!
A colony of termites can
chew up a whole house.

# Tick

Look on that deer.
What do you see?

The tick that you see is tiny.
It looks like a raisin with legs.
Do not touch one.
A tick sucks your blood.
It can make you sick.

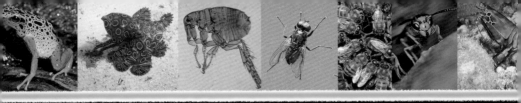

# DANGER! Deadly Animals Comprehension Questions

1. Why do you think the blue poison dart frog was given its name?

2. How long is the blue-ringed octopus?

3. Do you think a flea would be easy to see?

4. Why should you not touch a flea?

5. What does a fly use to taste?

6. What is a hornet nest shaped like?

7. When does the puffer fish puff up?

8. Why should you not eat a puffer fish?

9. What does a sea anemone look like?

10. Why should you not keep termites in your house?